FLAT-PACK

✵

FLAT-PACK

✦

ANNEY BOLGIANO

NEW MICHIGAN PRESS
TUCSON, ARIZONA

NEW MICHIGAN PRESS

DEPT OF ENGLISH, P. O. BOX 210067

UNIVERSITY OF ARIZONA

TUCSON, AZ 85721-0067

<http://newmichiganpress.com>

Orders and queries to <nmp@thediagram.com>.

ISBN 978-1-934832-84-4. FIRST PRINTING.

Design by Ander Monson.

Cover image by Anney Bolgiano.

CONTENTS

"Early on in the crisis, I picked up Marcus Aurelius and for the first time in my life read his *Meditations* not as an academic exercise, nor in the pursuit of pleasure, but with the same attitude I bring to the instructions for a flat-pack table—I was in need of practical assistance."

—Zadie Smith, *Intimations*

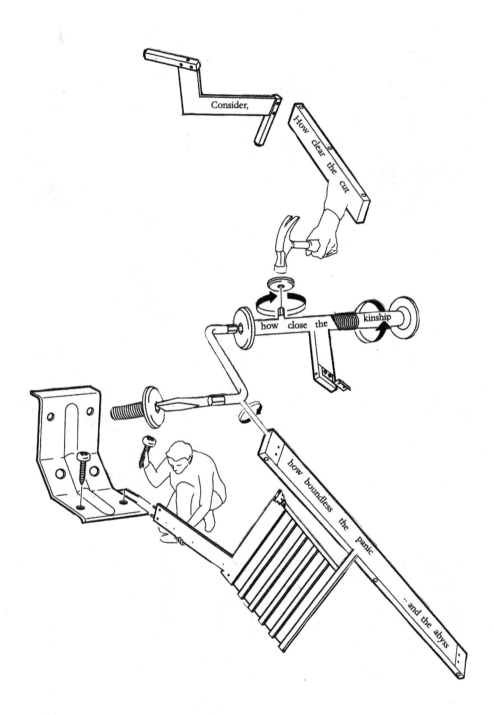

Consider,

How clear the cut

how close the kinship

how boundless the panic

– and the abyss

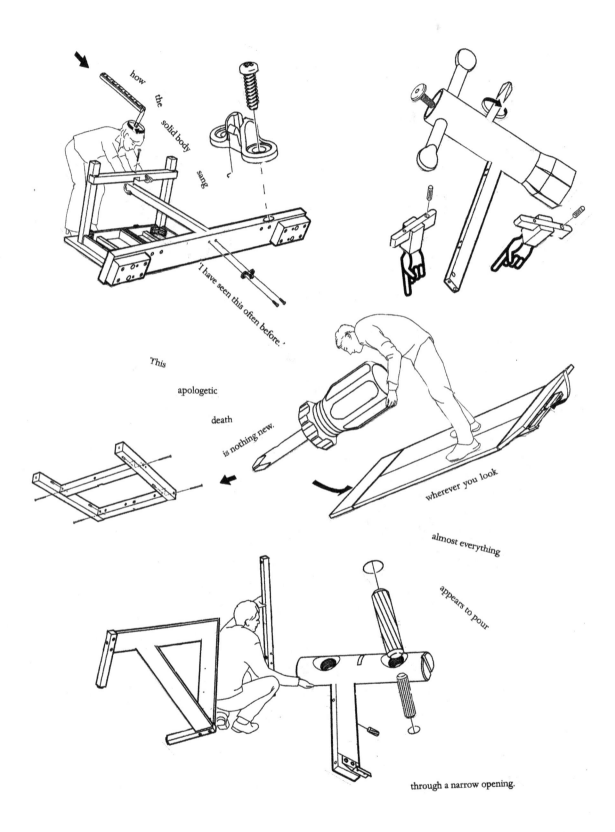

how the solid body sang

'I have seen this often before.'

This

apologetic

death

is nothing new.

wherever you look

almost everything

appears to pour

through a narrow opening.

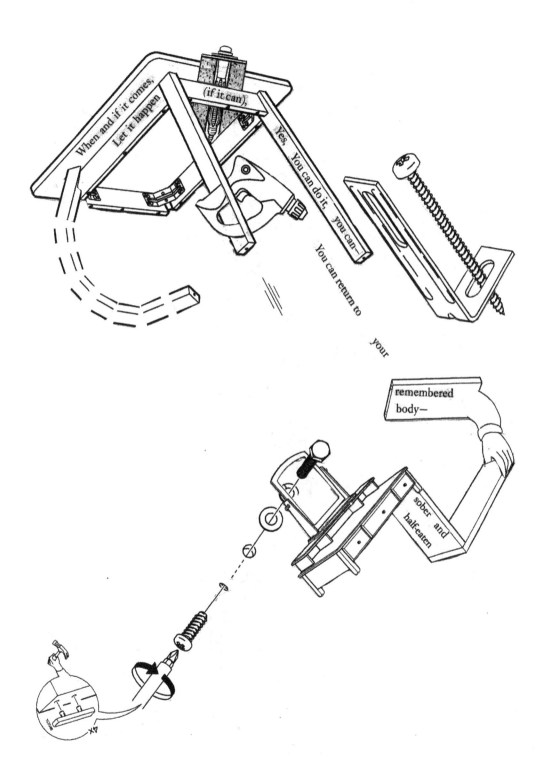

When and if it comes,

Let it happen

(if it can),

Yes, You can do it, You can—

You can—

You can return to

your

remembered body—

sober and half-eaten

clear-headed animate soul,

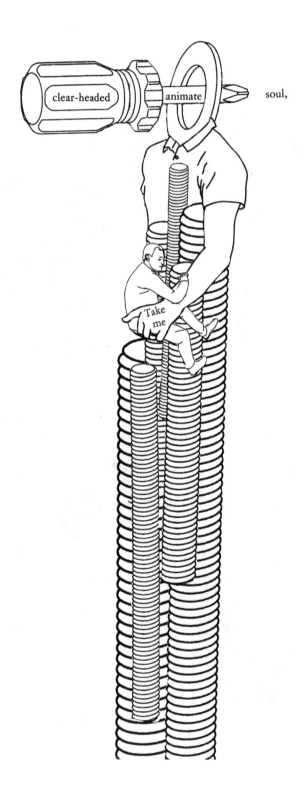

Take me

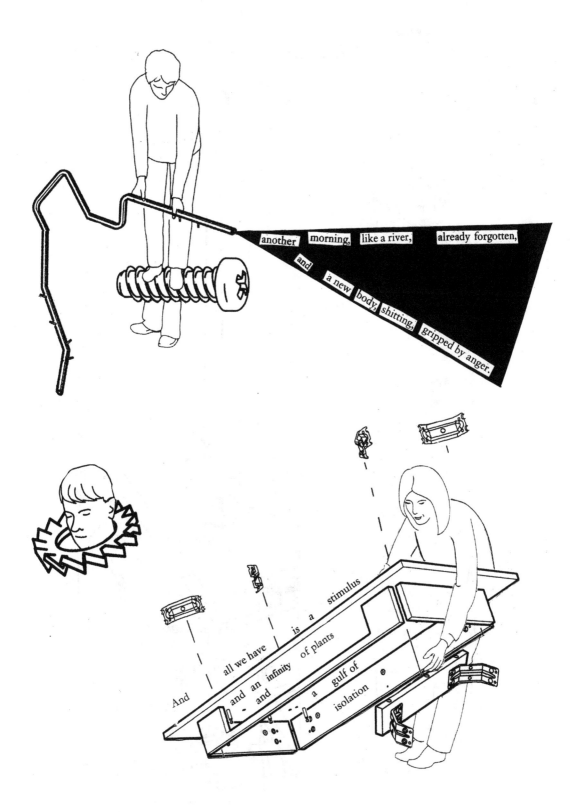

another morning, like a river, already forgotten, and a new body, shitting, gripped by anger.

And all we have is a stimulus and an infinity of plants and a gulf of isolation

My only fear

is

doing

anything

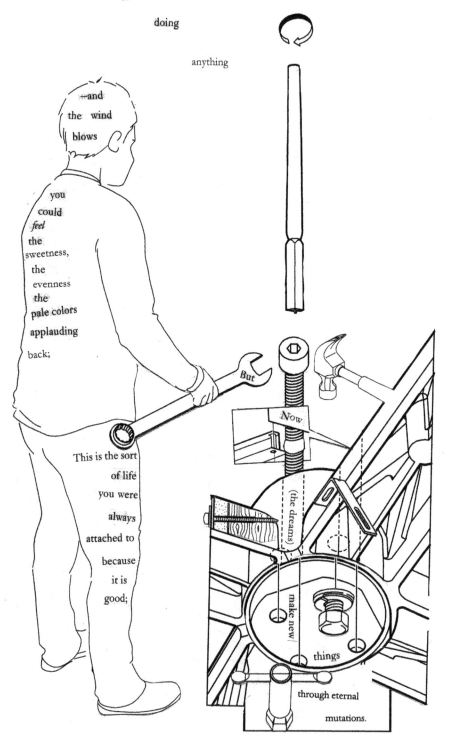

—and
the wind
blows

you
could
feel
the
sweetness,
the
evenness
the
pale colors
applauding
back;

But

Now

This is the sort
of life
you were
always
attached to
because
it is
good;

(the dreams)

make new

things

through eternal
mutations.

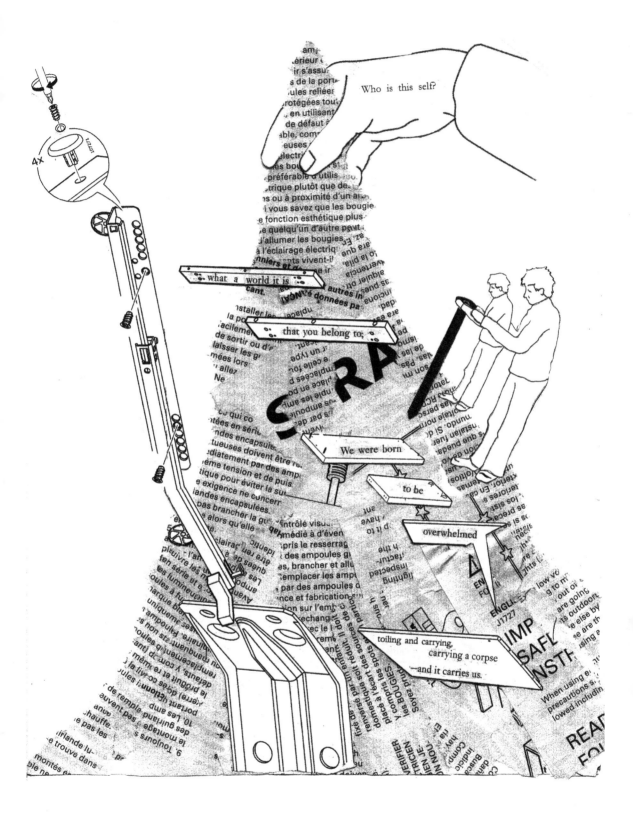

Who is this self?

what a world it is

that you belong to,

We were born

to be

overwhelmed

toiling and carrying,
carrying a corpse
—and it carries us.

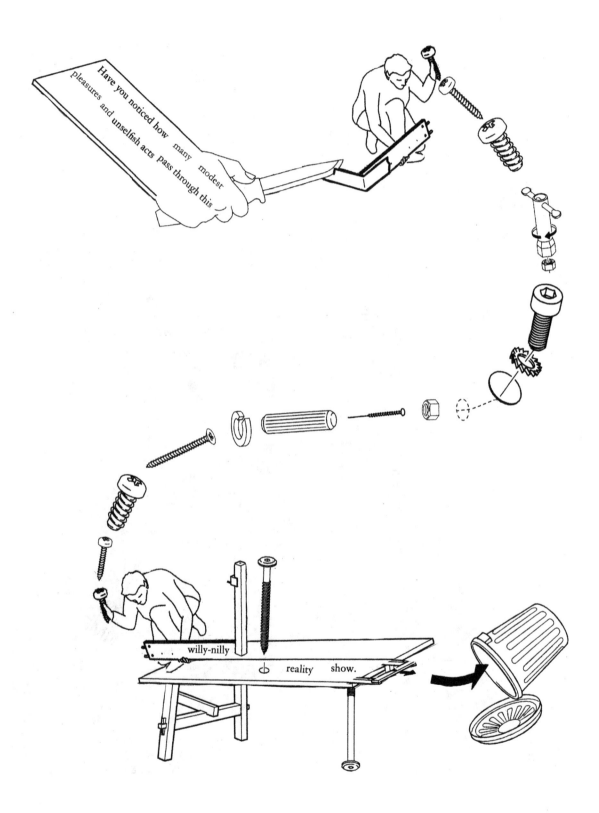

Have you noticed how many modest pleasures and unselfish acts pass through this

willy-nilly

reality show.

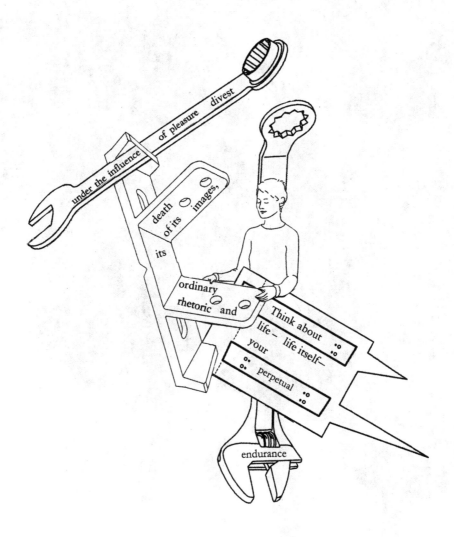

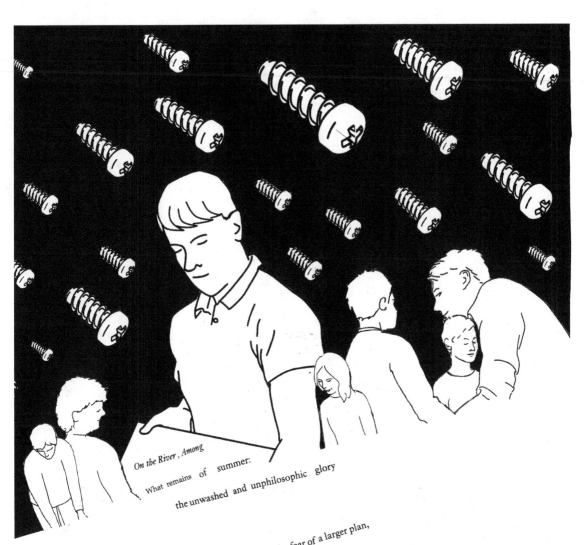

On the River , Among

What remains of summer:

the unwashed and unphilosophic glory

people are wrestling with the fear of a larger plan,

the fear that everything was born to forgive

First, tragedies, then warfare, And above all, the body,

In the end, they are loved by it—

and it doesn't hurt

the idea of wanting to feel affection for people to become a new person a different kind of failure burst open —as if you've lost control— as if you're blood in a bag as if the ever closer approach of freedom And "sanity" was greater than any handful of epithets but That's what we're talking about here

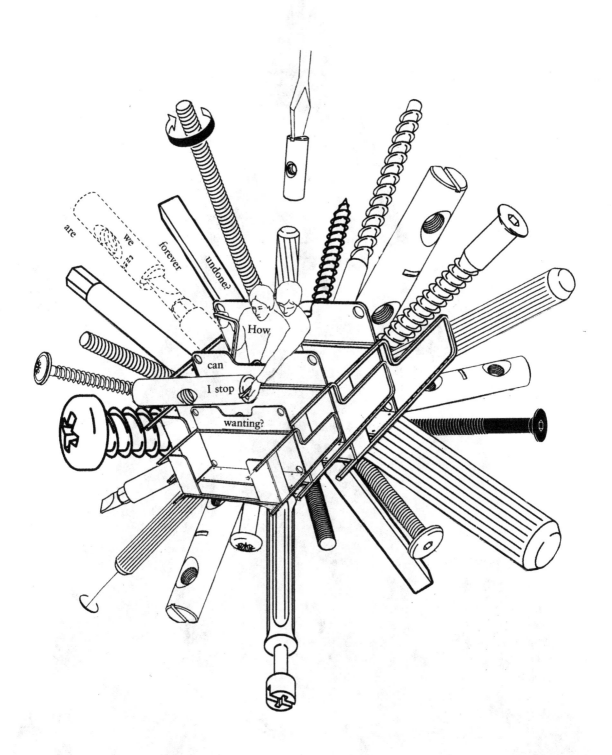

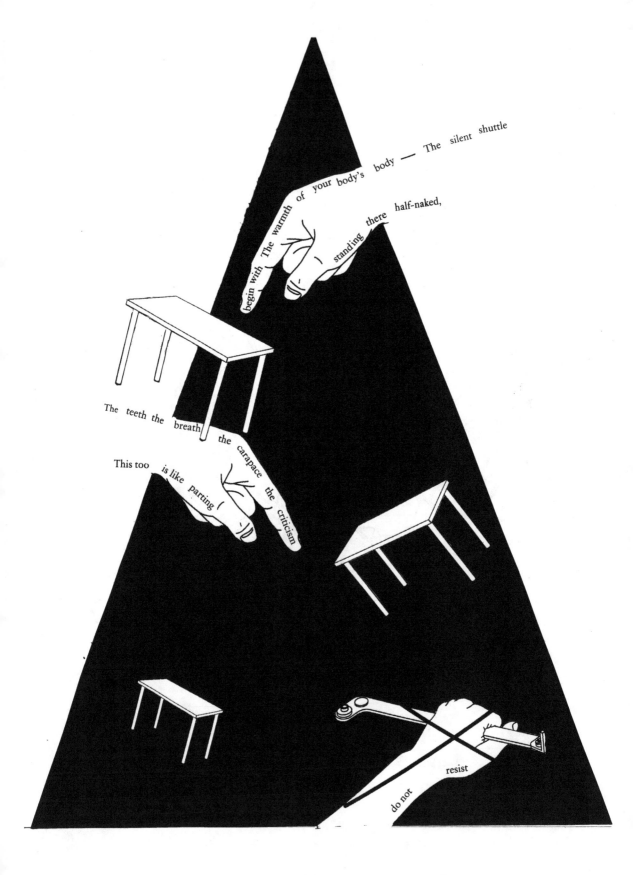

pain: the thing itself

how many
How many
how many
How many
How many
 have died,

and

How

many

pried

away

from

life

in

a single

motion.

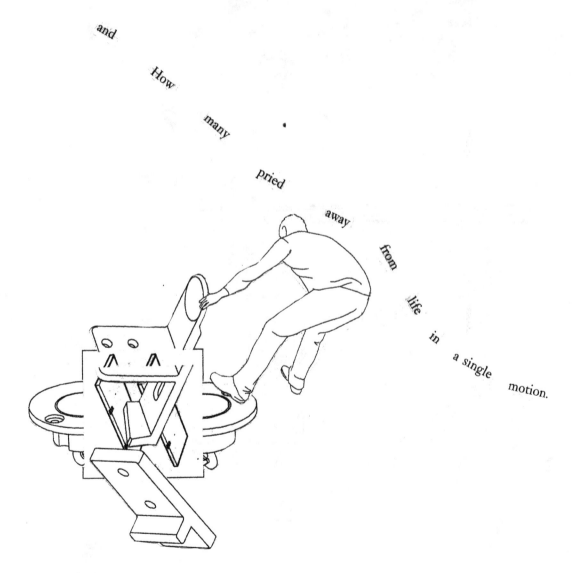

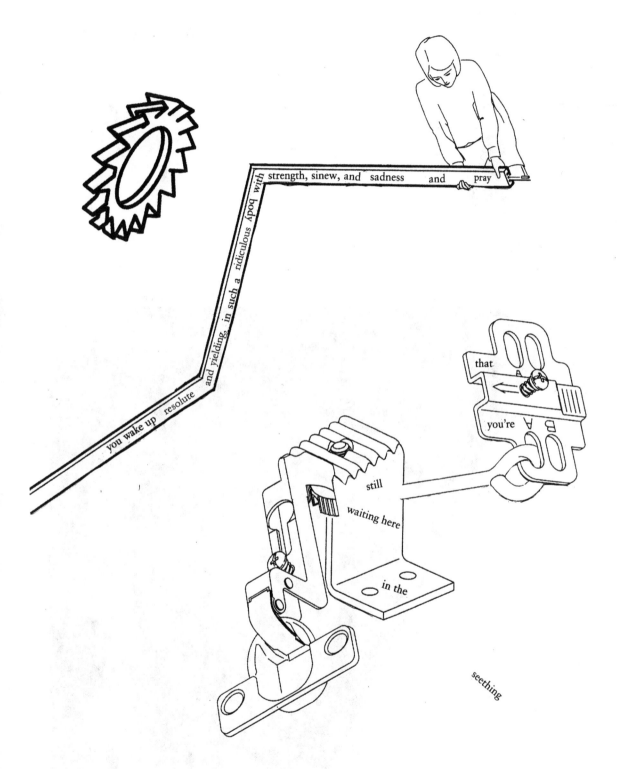

strength, sinew, and sadness and pray body with ridiculous a such in yielding, and resolute wake up you

that you're still waiting here in the seething

waters

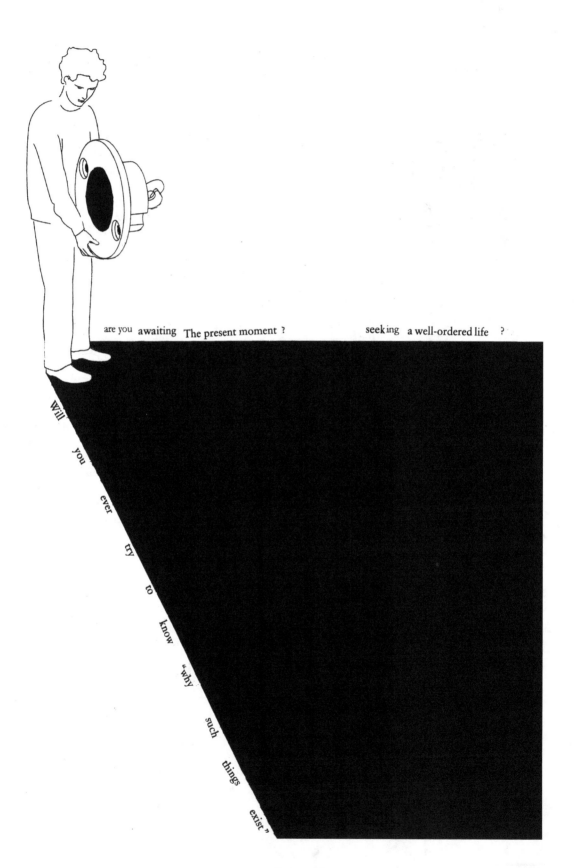

are you awaiting The present moment ?   seeking a well-ordered life   ?

Will

you

ever

try

to

know

"why

such

things

exist "

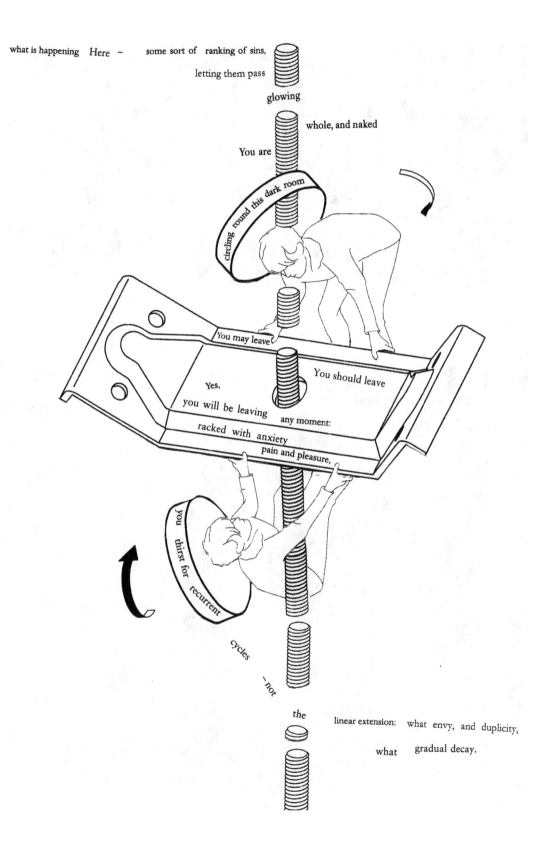

what is happening   Here –   some sort of ranking of sins,

letting them pass

glowing

whole, and naked

You are

circling round this dark room

You may leave

You should leave

Yes,

you will be leaving   any moment:

racked with anxiety

pain and pleasure,

you   thirst for   recurrent

cycles

–not

the

linear extension: what envy, and duplicity,

what   gradual decay.

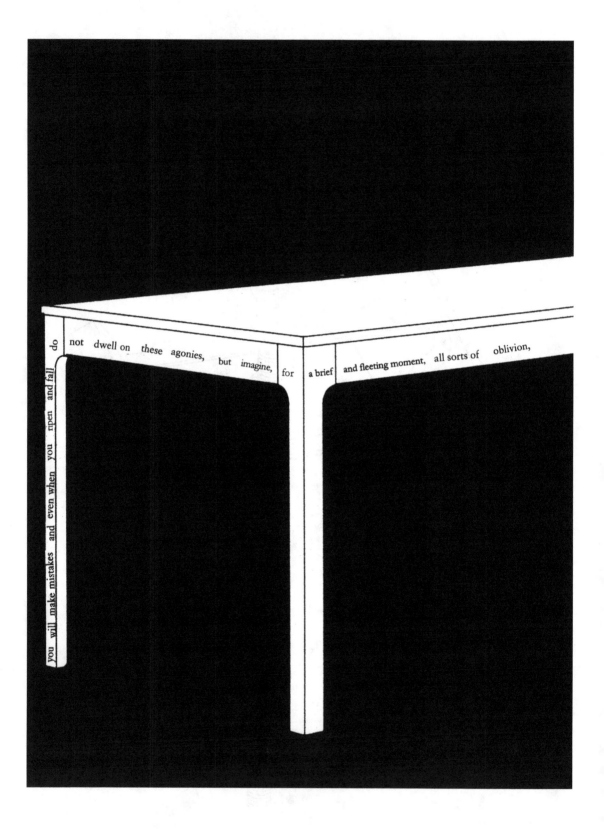

do not dwell on these agonies, but imagine, for a brief and fleeting moment, all sorts of oblivion,

you will make mistakes and even when you ripen and fall

of universal dissolution, of outright beauty ... and imagine that the rhythm of tolerance is a kind of community and you belong to it.

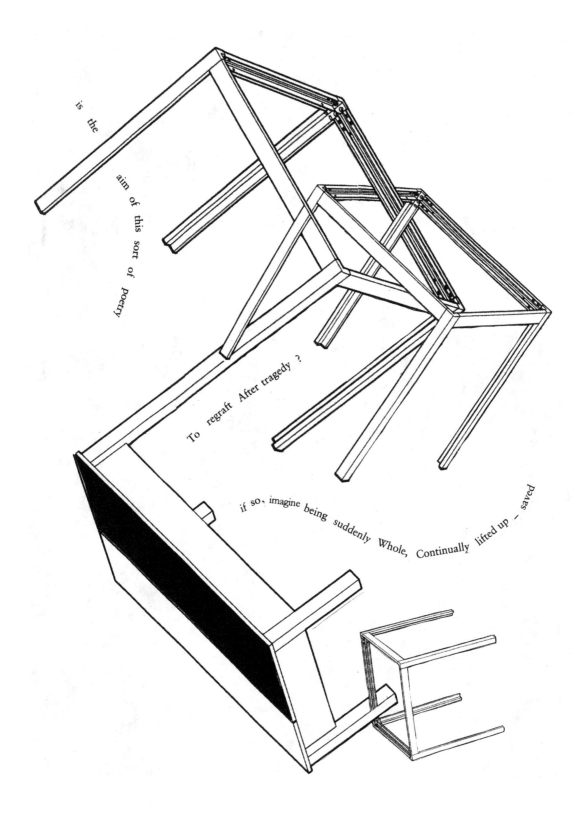

is the

aim of this sort of poetry

To regraft After tragedy ?

if so, imagine being suddenly Whole, Continually lifted up – saved

what is pain?

it might be   a procession, The empty pomp   of

The sun

pouring

itself

down

amid

all this

and

The light of a

timely end

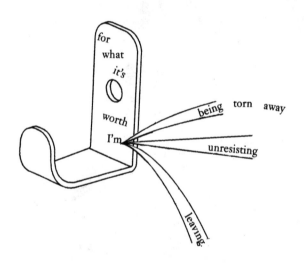

for
what
it's

worth

I'm → being torn away

unresisting

leaving.

NOTES

Source for collage images:

Various Flat-Pack Table Assembly Instructions, Inter-IKEA Systems B.V.

Sources for pulled text:

Aurelius, Marcus. *Meditations*. Translated by Martin Hammond, Penguin Books Ltd, 2014.

Aurelius, Marcus. *Meditations: A New Translation, with an Introduction, by Gregory Hays*. Translated by Gregory Hays, Modern Library, 2002.

Aurelius, Marcus. *Meditations*. Translated by George Long, CreateSpace Independent Publishing Platform, 2017.

ACKNOWLEDGEMENTS

Grateful acknowledgement is made to the editors of the following journals in which these poems first appeared:

"Pain: The Thing Itself," "My Only Fear," "Whoever Buries You," "When and If It Comes," "Who Is This Self": *CTRL + V*
"Consider How Clear," "How the Solid Body," "What Is Pain": *DIAGRAM*

I am also grateful for the help and encouragement of family, friends, and housemates, and to Art Farm Nebraska for giving me a special place to write and think.

ANNEY BOLGIANO lives in Washington, DC, where she teaches first year writing at Howard University and George Washington University. She holds an MFA from George Mason University and a BA from Guilford College. You can find more of her work in *TriQuarterly, DIAGRAM, The Rupture, Nashville Review, Salamander, Thin Air, A Velvet Giant, The Figure One, Frances House, Funny Looking Dog Quarterly*, and elsewhere. She is a Pushcart Prize Nominee, and a past resident of Art Farm Nebraska.

❋

COLOPHON

Text is set in a digital version of Jenson, designed by Robert Slimbach in 1996, and based on the work of punchcutter, printer, and publisher Nicolas Jenson. The titles here are in Futura.

NEW MICHIGAN PRESS, based in Tucson, Arizona, prints poetry and prose chapbooks, especially work that transcends traditional genre. Together with DIAGRAM, NMP sponsors a yearly chapbook competition.

DIAGRAM, a journal of text, art, and schematic, is published bimonthly at THEDIAGRAM.COM. Periodic print anthologies are available from the New Michigan Press at NEWMICHIGANPRESS.COM.

CPSIA information can be obtained
at www.ICGtesting.com
Printed in the USA
JSHW030005300322
24359JS00003B/38

9 781934 832844

Flat-Pack is a wonderfully original collage of text and image. Disembodied hands grapple with hammers; human figures fumble with puzzling tasks, tools and questions: "Are you awaiting the present moment? seeking a well-ordered life?" With its mash-up of modern anxiety and stoic wisdom, *Flat-Pack* manages to be harrowing, comforting and comic all at once. —SARAH J. SLOAT

$9.00 • IMAGE / TEXT
NEWMICHIGANPRESS.COM